T0078442

GOD'S COMMANDS

COMPILED
BY
OMAR BAGASRA
AND
ASSIYA DESOKY

authorHOUSE®

AuthorHouse™
1663 Liberty Drive
Bloomington, IN 47403
www.authorhouse.com
Phone: 833-262-8899

Published by AuthorHouse 12/08/2020

ISBN: 978-1-6655-1058-5 (sc)
ISBN: 978-1-6655-1057-8 (e)

Library of Congress Control Number: 2020924760

Print information available on the last page.

INTRODUCTION

This short book is to introduce Muslims, especially the young Muslims to Islam. In the modern time where internet and the social media has taken the central stage and the young Muslims looking for guidance ask *Siri*, Alexa, and other voice activated devices for answers. We are becoming dependent on the answers provided by the Search Engines or the voice activated devices, and we believe their answers as the truth. The answers are generated by "Artificial Intelligence" or AI. These devices are based on mathematical algorithms. The people behind the AI and algorithms are not qualified to correctly answer the questions that require deep understanding of the Qur'anic laws, the Holy Scriptures. The Qur'anic Arabic is over 1,4000 years old and there are few linguistics and scholars who may be able to transliterate the words of God, definitely not the AI of any kind of voice activated algorithm.

This small book provides a much-needed resource for those who are looking for the guidance from Qur'an. The commands of God- spelled out in the Holly Book in the clear manner.

We pray to God that this will serve as the lightning-rod for those who are seeking the TRUTH.

Assiya Desoky
Omar Bagasra

CONTENTS

1. Eman (absolute belief on Allah's Commands) 1
2. Manner of Listening to the Words of Allah 3
3. Patients in Adversity 4
4. Dawah (Call to Allah's way) 5
5. Haram and Halal 6
6. Manner of Ablution before the Prayers 8
7. Fasting 9
8. Rules of War 11
9. Truthfulness as a Witness 12
10. Obey God and His Apostle 13
11. This World is a place of trial 14
12. All True Believers will be in Paradise 15
13. Jihad is an Obligation 16
14. Keep your Covenants 18
15. Witness to the Last Will 19
16. Do not collaborate with Enemies 20
17. God Consciousness 22
18. Do not Enter others Houses without Permission ... 23
19. Rules of Social Manners & Modesty 24
20. Turn to God's Forgiveness for your Sins 25
21. The Right Way to deal with Social Discord 26

22. Do Not Spy on one each another and speak ill of others 27
23. Do you profess that which you do not practice! 28
24. Secret of Success 29
25. Do not let the worldly goods consume your soul... 30
26. Your worldly goods and your children are but a trial and a temptation! 32
27. Laws Concerning Fair Treatment of Wife 33
28. No Intimacy during Menstruation 34
29. Laws of Marriage & Divorce 35
30. Hijab 38
31. What God Almighty Has Forbidden to You 39
32. Do not Cheat your Business Partners 41
33. Guard Yourself from Fire 42
34. Infanticide is forbidden 43
35. Adultery is forbidden 44
36. Killing of Innocent People is forbidden 45
37. Give the Best in Charity 48
38. Judge others with Justice 49
39. Protect the possessions of Orphans 51
40. Pay for Both Men and Woman 53
41. A Man's Duty for a Woman 54
42. Pray only when you are AWARE! 55
43. Alcohol and Gambling is Forbidden 56
44. Observe Prayers and Pay Zakat (charity) 57
45. Life of this world is made to look good 59
46. Charity is Mandatory 60
47. Be Clear in your Heart about the Truth 61
48. Usury and Interest on Loans are forbidden 62
49. God alone who grants life and deals death 63

50. Do to grieve for the deniers of Truth...................... 64
51. There are Signs of His Manifestation Everywhere......65
52. Prayers 66
53. Surrender to God... 68

EMAN (ABSOLUTE BELIEF ON ALLAH'S COMMANDS)

In the name of God, The Most Gracious, The Dispenser of Grace:

Alif, Lam, Mim. This is the book of God, there is no doubt in it; it is a guidance for the God conscious for those who believe in the existence of that which is beyond the reach of human perception, and are constant in prayer, and spend on others out of what We provide for them as sustenance, who believe in what has been revealed to you and what was revealed before you and have firm faith in the hereafter (2:1-4).

GOD - there is no deity save Him, the Ever-Living, the Self-Subsistent Fount of All Being. Neither slumber overtakes Him, nor sleep. His is all that is in the heavens and all that is on earth. Who is there that could intercede with Him, unless it be by His leave?

He knows all that lies open before men and all that is hidden from them, whereas they cannot attain to aught of His knowledge save that which He wills [them to attain].

His eternal power overspreads the heavens and the earth, and their upholding wearies Him not. And he alone is truly exalted, tremendous (2:255).

MANNER OF LISTENING TO THE WORDS OF ALLAH

So, when the Quran is recited, listen carefully to it, and listen in silence, so that you might be graced with [God's] mercy (7:204).

PATIENTS IN ADVERSITY

O YOU who have attained to faith! Seek aid in steadfast patience and prayer: for, behold, God is with those who are patient in adversity (2:153).

And most certainly shall We try you by means of danger, and hunger, and loss of worldly goods, of lives and of [labor's] fruits. But give glad tidings unto those who are patient in adversity - who, when calamity befalls them, say, "Verily, unto God do we belong and, verily, unto Him we shall return." It is they upon whom their Sustainer's blessings and grace are bestowed, and it is they, they who are rightly guided (2:155-157).

O you who have attained to faith! Be patient in adversity, and vie in patience with one another, and be ever ready [to do what is right], and remain conscious of God, so that you might attain to a happy state (3:200)!

DAWAH (CALL TO ALLAH'S WAY)

CALL THOU (all mankind] unto thy Sustainer's path with wisdom and goodly exhortation, and argue with them in the most kindly manner for, behold, your Sustainer knows best as to who strays from His path, and best knows He as to who are the right-guided. Hence, if you have to respond to an attack (in argument], respond only to the extent of the attack levelled against you; but to bear yourselves with patience is indeed far better for (you, since God is with] those who are patient in adversity (16:125-126).

Haram and Halal

FORBIDDEN to you is carrion, and blood, and the flesh of swine, and that over which any name other than God's has been invoked, and the animal that has been strangled, or beaten to death, or killed by a fall, or gored to death, or savaged by a beast of prey, save that which you [yourselves] may have slaughtered while it was still alive; and [forbidden to you is] all that has been slaughtered on idolatrous altars (5:3).

And [you are forbidden] to seek to learn through divination what the future may hold in store for you: this is sinful conduct.

Today, those who are bent on denying the truth have lost all hope of [your ever forsaking] your religion: do not, then, hold them in awe, but stand in awe of Me!

Today have I perfected your religious law for you, and have bestowed upon you the full measure of My blessings, and willed that self-surrender unto Me (meaning Islam) shall be your religion.

As for him, however, who is driven [to what is forbidden] by dire necessity and not by an inclination to sinning - behold, God is much-forgiving, a dispenser of grace.

They will ask you as to what is lawful to them. Say: Lawful to you are all the clean things of life. And as for those hunting animals which you train by imparting to them something of the knowledge that God has imparted to yourselves - eat of what they seize for you, but mention God's name over it and remain conscious of God: verily, God is swift in reckoning.

Today, all the good things of life have been made lawful to you. And the food of the People of the Book is lawful to you, and your food is lawful to them. And [lawful to you are], in wedlock, women from among those who believe [in this divine writ], and, in wedlock, women from among those who have received Book before you, provided that you give them their dowers, taking them in honest wedlock, not in fornication, nor as secret love-companions.

The work of he who refuses to follow the way of faith will go to waste, and he will be among the utter losers in the Hereafter.

MANNER OF ABLUTION
BEFORE THE PRAYERS

O YOU who have attained to faith! When you are about to pray, wash your face, and your hands and arms up to the elbows, and pass your [wet] hands lightly over your head, and [wash] your feet up to the ankles. And if you are in a state requiring total ablution, purify yourselves. But if you are ill, or are travelling, or have just satisfied a want of nature, or have cohabited with a woman, and can find no water - then take resort to pure dust, passing therewith lightly over your face and your hands. God does not want to impose any hardship on you, but wants to make you pure, and to bestow upon you the full measure of His blessings, so that you might have cause to be grateful (5:6).

FASTING

O YOU who have attained to faith! Fasting is ordained for you as it was ordained for those before you, so that you might remain conscious of God: Fasting is for a fixed number of days, and if one of you be sick, or if one of you be on a journey, you will fast the same number of other days later on. For those who are capable of fasting (but still do not fast) there is redemption: feeding a needy man for each day missed. And whoever does more good than he is bound to do does good unto himself thereby; for to fast is to do good unto yourselves - if you but knew it (2:183-184).

It was the month of Ramadan in which the Qur'an was [first] bestowed from on high as a guidance unto man and a self-evident proof of that guidance, and as the standard by which to discern the true from the false. Hence, whoever of you lives to see this month shall fast throughout it; but he that is ill, or on a journey, [shall fast instead for the same] number of other days. God wills that you shall have ease, and does not will you to suffer hardship; but [He desires] that you complete the number [of days required], and that you extol God for His having guided you aright, and give thanks to Him (2:185).

IT IS lawful for you to go in unto your wives during the night preceding the [day's] fast: they are as a garment for you, and you are as a garment for them. God is aware that you would have deprived yourselves of this right, and so He has turned unto you in His mercy and removed this hardship from you. Now, then, you may lie with them skin to skin, and avail yourselves of that which God has ordained for you, and eat and drink until you can discern the white streak of dawn against the blackness of night, and then resume fasting until nightfall; but do not lie with them skin to skin when you are about to abide in meditation in houses of worship (2:187).

RULES OF WAR

[H ence,] O you who have attained to faith, when you go forth in the way of God, ascertain and distinguish (between friend and foe), and do not say to him who offers you the greeting of peace: "You are not a believer." If you seek the good of this worldly life, there lies with God abundant gain. After all, you too were such before, but then God was gracious to you. Discern then, for God is well aware of what you do (4:94).

Those believers who sit at home, unless they do so out of a disabling injury, are not the equals of those who strive in the way of God with their possessions and their lives. God has exalted in rank those who strive with their possessions and their lives over those who sit at home; this even though to each God has promised some good reward, he has preferred for a mighty reward those who strive (in the way of Allah) over those who sit at home. For them are ranks, forgiveness, and favors from him. God is all-forgiving, all-compassionate (4:95-96).

TRUTHFULNESS AS A WITNESS

B elievers! Be upholders of justice, and bearers of witness to truth for the sake of God, even though it may be against yourselves or against your parents and kinsmen, or the rich or the poor, for God is more concerned with their well-being then you are. Do not, then follow your own desires lest you keep away from justice. If you twist or turn away from (the truth), know that God is well aware of all that you do (4:135).

Obey God and His Apostle

B elievers! Believe in God and his messenger and in the book, he has revealed to his messenger, and in the book, he revealed before. And whoever disbelievers in God, in his angels, in his books, in his messengers and in the last day, has indeed strayed far away (4:136).

O YOU who have attained to faith! Remain conscious of God, and believe in His Apostle, [and] He will grant you doubly of His grace, and will light for you a light wherein you shall walk, and will forgive you [your past sins]: for God is much-forgiving, a dispenser of grace (57:28).

THIS WORLD IS A PLACE OF TRIAL

(O Messenger), do not let the strutting about of the unbelievers in the land deceive you. This is but a trifling and fleeting enjoyment; then their destination is Hell – what an evil resting place! whereas those who remain conscious of their Sustainer shall have gardens through which running waters flow, therein to abide: a ready welcome from God. And that which is with God is best for the truly virtuous (3:196-198).

ALL TRUE BELIEVERS WILL
BE IN PARADISE

A mong the People of the Book some believe in God and what has been revealed to you, and what has been revealed to them. They humble themselves before God, and do not sell Allah's revelations for a trivial gain. For such their reward lies with their Lord. God is swift in reckoning (3:199).

Jihad is an Obligation

O MANKIND! A manifestation of the truth has now come unto you from your Sustainer, and We have sent down unto you a clear light. God will surely admit those who believe in him and hold fast to him to his mercy and bounty and will guide them on to a straight way to himself (4:174-175).

Believers! Obey God and his messenger and do not turn away from him after you hear his command. And do not be like those who say: "We hear," though they do not hearken (8:20-21).

Believers! Respond to God, and respond to the messenger when he calls you to that which gives you life. Know well that God stands between a person and his heart, and it is to him that all of you shall be mustered (8:24).

Believers! When you encounter a host in a battle, stand firm and remember God much that you may triumph (8:45).

O you who have attained to faith! Fight against those deniers of the truth who are near you, and let them find you adamant; and know that God is with those who are conscious of Him (9:123).

Believers, whenever you encounter a hostile force of unbelievers, do not turn your backs to them in flight. For he who turns his back on them on such an occasion except that it be for tactical reasons or turning to join another company – he shall incur the wrath of God and Hell shall be his abode. It is an evil destination (8:15-16).

Keep your Covenants

O YOU who have attained to faith! Be true to your covenants! All grazing beasts of the flock are permitted to you except those which are recited to you hereafter; but you are not allowed to hunt in the state of ihram (the state of Pilgrim Sanctity). Indeed God decrees as he wills (5:1).

WITNESS TO THE LAST WILL

B elievers! When death approaches you, let two persons of equity among you act as witnesses when you make your bequest; or let two of those from others than yourselves act as witnesses if you are on a journey when the affliction of death befalls you. Then if any doubt occurs you shall detain both of them (in the mosque) after the prayer, and they shall swear by Allah: "We shall neither sell our testimony in return for any gain even though it concerns any near of kin nor shall we conceal our testimony which we owe to God, for then we should become among the sinners (5:106)."

Do not collaborate with Enemies

Believers! Do not be unfaithful to God and the messenger, nor be knowingly unfaithful to your trusts. and know that your worldly goods and your children are but a trial and a temptation, and that with God there is a tremendous reward (8:27-28).

O YOU who have attained to faith! Do not take your fathers and your brothers for allies if a denial of the truth is dearer to them than faith: for those of you who ally themselves with them - it is they, they who are evildoers (9:23)!

Believers, do not make friends with those against whom God is wrathful and who are despaired of the hereafter, as despaired as are the unbelievers lying in their graves (60:13).

who take the unbelievers for their allies in preference to the believers. Do they seek honor from them whereas honor altogether belongs to God alone? God has enjoined upon you in the Book that when you hear the Signs of God being rejected and scoffed at, you will not sit with them until they engage in some other talk, or else you will become like them. Know well, God will gather the hypocrites and the unbelievers in Hell – all together. These hypocrites watch you closely: if victory is granted to you by God, they will say: "Were we not with you?" And were the unbelievers to gain the upper hand, they will say: "Did we not have mastery over you, and yet we protected you from the believers?" It is God Who will judge between you on the Day of Resurrection, and He will not allow the unbelievers, in any way, to gain advantage over the believers (4:139-141).

Believers! Do not take for your allies those who make a mockery and sport of your faith, be they those given the Book before you or other unbelievers. Fear God if you indeed believe. And when you are called to pray, they take it for a mockery and sport. That because they are a people who do not understand (5:57-58).

GOD CONSCIOUSNESS

O YOU who have attained to faith! Remain conscious of God, and be among those who are true to their word (9:119)!

And say: The truth has now come [to light], and falsehood has withered away: for, behold, all falsehood is bound to wither away (17:81)!"

Believers, fear God and let every person look to what he sends forward for the marrow. Fear Allah; God is well aware of all that you do (59:18).

So, hold God in awe as much as you can, and listen and obey, and be charitable. This is for your own good. And whoever remains safe from his own greediness, it is such that will prosper (64:16).

Do not Enter others Houses without Permission

Believers! Enter not houses other than your own houses until you have obtained the permission of the inmates of those houses and have greeted them with peace. This is better for you. It is expected that you will observe this (24:27).

Rules of Social Manners & Modesty

B elievers! At three times let those whom your right hands possess and those of your children who have not yet reached puberty ask leave of you before entering your quarters: before the morning prayer and when you take off your clothes at noon, and after the night prayer. These are the three times of privacy for you. If they come to you at other times then there is no sin for them nor for you, for you have to visit one another frequently. Thus, does God clearly explain his directives to you. God is all-knowing, all-wise (24:58).

Turn to God's Forgiveness for your Sins

Know, then, [O man,] that there is no deity save God, and [while there is yet time,] ask forgiveness for your sins and for [the sins of] all other believing men and women: for God knows the places where you move about and where you dwell (47:19).

Believers, turn to God in sincere repentance; maybe your Lord will expunge your evil deeds and admit you to the Gardens beneath which rivers flow. This will be on the Day when God will not disgrace the Prophet and those who have embraced faith and are with him; their light will be running before them and on their right hands, and they will say: "Our Lord, perfect for us our light and forgive us. Surely You have power over everything (66:8)."

THE RIGHT WAY TO DEAL WITH SOCIAL DISCORD

Believers, let not a group (of men) scoff at another group, it may well be that the latter (at whom they scoff) are better than they; nor let group of woman scoff at another group, it may well be that the latter are better than they. And do not taunt one another, nor revile one another by nicknames. It is an evil thing to gain notoriety for ungodliness after belief. Those who do not repent are indeed the wrong doers (49:11).

DO NOT SPY ON ONE
EACH ANOTHER AND
SPEAK ILL OF OTHERS

O you who have attained to faith! Avoid most guesswork [about one another] - for, behold, some of [such] guesswork is [in itself] a sin; and do not spy upon one another, and neither allow yourselves to speak ill of one another behind your backs. Would any of you like to eat the flesh of his dead brother? Nay, you would loathe it! And be conscious of God. Verily, God is an acceptor of repentance, a dispenser of grace (49:12)!

DO YOU PROFESS THAT WHICH YOU DO NOT PRACTICE!

Believers, why do you profess that which you do not practice? It is most loathsome in the sight of God that you should profess what you do not practice (61:2-3).

SECRET OF SUCCESS

O YOU who have attained to faith! Shall I point out to you a bargain that will save you from grievous suffering [in this world and in the life to come]? You are to believe in God and His Apostle, and to strive hard in God's cause with your possessions and your lives: this is for your own good - if you but knew it (61:10-11)!

He will forgive you your sins, and [in the life to come] will admit you into gardens through which running rivers flow, and into goodly mansions in [those] gardens of perpetual bliss: that [will be] the triumph supreme! And He will grant you yet other favor that you dearly love: help from God [in this world], and a victory soon to come: and [thereof, O Prophet,] give glad tiding to all who believe (61:12-13).

DO NOT LET THE WORLDLY GOODS CONSUME YOUR SOUL

B elievers, let your possessions and your offspring not make you negligent of Allah's remembrance. For whoso does that, they will be the losers. And spend of what God has granted you by way of sustenance before death should come to any of you and he should say: "Lord, why did you not defer my return for a while so that I might give alms and be among the righteous (63:9-10)?"

O you who have attained to faith! Be conscious of God with all the consciousness that is due to Him, and see that you do not die save in submission to Him (3:102).

Hold fast together to the cable of God and be not divided. Remember the blessing that God bestowed upon you: you were once enemies, than He brought your hearts together, so that through His Blessing you became brothers. You stood on the brink of a pit of fire and He delivered you from it. Thus God makes His Signs clear to you that you may be guided to the Right Way. And from amongst you there must be a party who will call people to all that is good and will enjoin the doing of all that is right and will forbid the doing of all that is wrong. It is they who will attain true success (3:103-104).

Your worldly goods and your children are but a trial and a temptation!

Believers, there are enemies to you from among your spouses and your offspring, so beware of them. But if you forgive and overlook their offences and pardon them, then surely God is Most Forgiving, Most Compassionate. Your possessions and your offspring are nothing but a trial for you. And there awaits a great reward for you with Allah (64:14-15).

Laws Concerning Fair Treatment of Wife

And if a woman has reason to fear ill-treatment from her husband, or that he might turn away from her, it shall not be wrong for the two to set things peacefully to rights between themselves: for peace is best, and selfishness is ever-present in human souls. But if you do good and are conscious of Him - behold, God is indeed aware of all that you do (4:128).

And if husband and wife do separate, God shall provide for each of them out of His abundance: for God is indeed infinite, wise, and unto God belongs all that is in the heavens and all that is on earth (4:130-131).

No Intimacy during Menstruation

They ask you about the menstruation. Say: "It is a state of impurity; so keep away from women in the state of menstruation, and do not approach them until they are cleansed. And when they are cleansed, then come to them as God has commanded you." Truly, God loves those who abstain from evil and keep themselves pure (2:222).

LAWS OF MARRIAGE & DIVORCE

B elievers! It is not lawful for you to become heirs to women against their will. It is not lawful that you should put constraint upon them so that you may take away anything of what you have given them; (you may not put constraint upon them) unless they are guilty of brazenly immoral conduct. Live with your wives gracefully. If you dislike them in any manner, it may be that you dislike something in which God has placed much good for you (4:19).

And if you decide to dispense with a wife in order to take another, do not take away anything of what you might have given the first one, even if you had given her a heap of gold. Would you take it back by slandering her and committing a manifest wrong? How can you take it away after each one has enjoyed the other, and they have taken a firm covenant from you (4:20-21)?

AND DO NOT marry women whom your fathers have previously married - although what is past is past: this, verily, is a shameful deed, and a hateful thing, and an evil way (4:22).

Forbidden to you are your mothers, your daughters, your sisters, your father's sisters and your mother's sisters, your brother's daughters and your sister's daughters, your milk-mothers, your milk-sisters, the mothers of your wives, and the stepdaughters – who are your foster-children, born of your wives with whom you have consummated the marriage; but if you have not consummated the marriage with them, there will be no blame upon you (if you marry their daughters). It is also forbidden for you to take the wives of the sons who have sprung from your loins and to take two sisters together in marriage, although what is past is past. Surely God is All-Forgiving, All Compassionate (4:23).

Also forbidden to you are all married women (muhsanat) except those women whom your right hands have come to possess (as a result of war). This is Allah's decree and it is binding upon you. But it is lawful for you to seek out all women except these, offering them your wealth and the protection of wedlock rather than using them for the unfettered satisfaction of lust. And give bridal-due of those whom you have enjoyed in wedlock as an obligation. But there is no blame on you if you mutually agree to alter the settlement after it has been made. Surely God is All-Knowing, All-wise (4:23).

And those of you who cannot afford to marry free, believing women (muhsanat), let them marry such believing women whom your right hands possess. God knows all about your faith. All of you belong to one another. Marry them, then, with the leave of their guardians, and give them their bridal-due in a fair manner that they may live in the protection of wedlock rather than be either mere objects of unfettered lust or given to secret love affairs. Then if they become guilty of immoral conduct after they have entered into wedlock, they shall be liable to half the penalty to which free women (muhsanat) are liable. This relaxation is for those of you who fear falling into sin by remaining unmarried. But if you preserve, it is better for you. God is All-Forgiving, All-Compassionate (4:23).

Hijab

TELL the believing men to lower their gaze and to be mindful of their chastity: this will be most conducive to their purity - [and,] verily, God is aware of all that they do (24:30).

And enjoin believing women to cast down their looks and guard their private parts and not reveal their adornment except that which is revealed of itself, and to draw their veils over their bosoms, and not to reveal their adornment save to their husbands, or their fathers, or the father of their husbands, or of their own sons, or the sons of their husbands, or their brothers, or the sons of their brother, or the sons of their sisters, or the women with whom they associate, or those that are in their bondage, or the male attendants in their service free of sexual interest, or boys that are yet unaware of illicit matters pertaining to women. Nor should they stamp their feet on the ground in such manner that their hidden ornament becomes revealed (24:31).

WHAT GOD ALMIGHTY HAS FORBIDDEN TO YOU

-

Say to them, (O Muhammad): "Come, let me recite what your Lord has forbidden:

(i)   That you associate nothing with Him;

(ii) And do good to your parents

(iii) And do not slay your children out of fear of poverty. We provide you and will likewise provide them with sustenance;

(iv) And do not even draw near to things shameful – be they open or secret;

(v)   And do not slay the soul sanctified by God except in just cause; this He has enjoined upon you so that you may understand;

(vi) and do not even draw near to the property of the orphan in his minority except in the best manner;

(vii) And give full measures and weight with justice, We do not burden anyone beyond his capacity;

(viii) When you speak, be just, even thought it concerns a near of kin;

(ix) And fulfil the covenant of Allah. That is what He has enjoined upon you so that you may take heed (6:151-152).

DO NOT CHEAT YOUR BUSINESS PARTNERS

Believers! Do not devour one another's possessions wrongfully; rather, let there be trading by mutual consent; and do not kill yourselves. Surely God is ever Compassionate to you. And whoever does this by way of transgression and injustice We shall surely cast him into the Fire; that indeed is quite easy for Allah (4:29-30).

If you avoid the great sins, which you have been enjoined to shun, we shall efface your [minor] bad deeds, and shall cause you to enter an abode of glory (4:31).

GUARD YOURSELF FROM FIRE

B elievers, guard yourselves and your kindred against a Fire whose fuel is human beings and stones, a Fire held in the charge of fierce and stern angels who never disobey what He has commanded them, and always do what they are bidden. (It will then be said): "Unbelievers, make no excuses today. You are being recompensed for nothing else but your deeds (66:6-7)."

Your Lord has decreed:

(i)   Do not worship any but Him;

(ii) Be good to your parents; and should both or any one of them attain old age with you, do not say to them even "fie" neither chide them, but speak to them with respect, and be humble and tender to them and say: "Lord, show mercy to them as they nurtured me when I was small (17:23-24)."

INFANTICIDE IS FORBIDDEN

Hence, do not kill your children for fear of poverty: it is We who shall provide sustenance for them as well as for you. Verily, killing them is a great sin (17:31).

ADULTERY IS FORBIDDEN

A nd do not commit adultery" - for, behold, it is an abomination and an evil way (17:32).

KILLING OF INNOCENT
PEOPLE IS FORBIDDEN

Do not kill any person whom God has forbidden to kill, except with right. We have granted the heir of him who has been wrongfully killed the authority to (claim retribution); so let him not exceed in slaying. He shall be helped (17:33).

Omar Bagasra and Assiya Desoky

PUT CONCISE LOAN CONTRACT
IN WRITING

Believers! Whenever you contract a debt from one another for a known term, commit it to writing. Let a scribe write it down between you justly, and the scribe may not refuse to write it down according to what God has taught him; so let him write, and let the debtor dictate; and let him fear God, his Lord, and curtail no part of it. If the debtor be feeble-minded, weak, or incapable of dictating, let his guardian dictate equitably, an call upon two of your men as witnesses; but if two men are not there, then let there be one man and two women as witnesses from among those acceptable to you so that if one of the two women should fail to remember, the other might remind her. Let not the witnesses refuse when they are summoned (to give evidence). Do not show slackness in writing down the transaction, whether small or large, along with the term of its payment. That is fairest in the sight of God; it is best for testimony and is more likely to exclude all doubts. If it be a matter of buying and selling on the spot, it is not blameworthy if you do not write it down; but do take witnesses when you settle commercial transactions with one another. And the scribe or the witness may be done no harm. It will be sinful if you do so. Beware of the wrath of God. He teaches you the Right Way and has full knowledge of everything. God knows whatever you spend or whatever you vow (to spend). The wrong-doers have none to succor them. If you dispense your charity publicly, it is well; but if you conceal it and pay it to the needy in secret, it will be even better for you. This will atone for several of your misdeeds. God is well aware of all that you do. You are not responsible for setting these people on the Right Way; God sets on the Right Way whomsoever He wills. Whatever wealth you spend in charity is to your own benefit for you spend merely to please God. So, whatever you spend in charity will be repaid to you in full and you shall not be wronged. Those needy ones who are wholly wrapped up in the cause of God, and who are hindered from moving about the earth in search of their livelihood, especially deserve help. He who is unaware of their circumstances supposes them to be wealthy because of their dignified bearing, but you will know them by their countenance, although they do not go about begging of people with importunity. Whatever wealth you spend on helping them, God will know of it. Those who spend their wealth by night and by day, secretly and publicly, will find that their reward is secure with their Lord and that there is no reason for them to entertain any fear or grief. As for those who devour interest, they behave as the one whom Satan has confounded with his touch. Seized in this state they say: "Buying and selling is but a kind of interest, even though God has made buying and selling lawful, and interest unlawful (2:282-275).

GIVE THE BEST IN CHARITY

O you who have attained to faith! Spend on others out of the good things which you may have acquired, and out of that which We bring forth for you from the earth; and choose not for your spending the bad things which you yourselves would not accept without averting your eyes in disdain. And know that God is self-sufficient, ever to be praised (2:267).

JUDGE OTHERS WITH JUSTICE

God commands you to deliver trusts to those worthy of them; and when you judge between people, judge with justice. Excellent is the admonition God gives you. God is All-Hearing, All-Seeing (4:58).

O YOU who have attained to faith! Be ever steadfast in your devotion to God, bearing witness to the truth in all equity; and never let hatred of anyone lead you into the sin of deviating from justice. Be just: this is closest to being God-conscious. And remain conscious of God: verily, God is aware of all that you do (5:8).

God has promised those who believe and do righteous deeds forgiveness from sins and a great reward. As for those who disbelieve and give the lie to Our Signs, they are destined for the Blazing Flame (5:9-10).

Believers! Fear God and seek the means to come near to Him, and strive hard in His Way; maybe you will attain true success. For those wo disbelieved – even if they had all that is in the earth, and the like of it with it and they had offered it all as ransom from chastisement on the Day of Resurrection, it will not be accepted of them. A painful chastisement lies in store for them. They will wish to come out of the Fire, but they will not. Theirs will be a long-lasting chastisement (5:35-37).

PROTECT THE POSSESSIONS OF ORPHANS

And do not even go near the property of the orphan – except that it be in the best manner – till he attains his maturity. And fulfil the covenant, for you will be called to account regarding the covenant (17:34).

Omar Bagasra and Assiya Desoky

SELL YOUR GOODS WITH HONESTY

And give full measure whenever you measure, and weigh with a balance that is true: this will be [for your own] good, and best in the end (17:35).

Pay for Both Men and Woman

Hence, do not covet the bounties which God has bestowed more abundantly on some of you than on others. Men shall have a benefit from what they earn, and women shall have a benefit from what they earn. Ask, therefore, God [to give you] out of His bounty: behold, God has indeed full knowledge of everything (4:32).

A Man's Duty for a Woman

Men are the protectors and maintainers of women because God has made one of them excel over the other, and because they spend out of their possessions (to support them). Thus righteous women are obedient and guard the rights of men in their absence under Allah's protection. And for women of whom you fear rebellion, admonish them, and remain apart from them in beds, and beat them. Then if they obey you, do not seek ways to harm them. God is the Exalted, the Great (4:34).

PRAY ONLY WHEN YOU ARE AWARE!

O YOU who have attained to faith! Do not draw near to the Prayer while you are intoxicated until you know what you are saying; nor when you are defiled – save when you are travelling – until you have washed yourselves. If you are either ill or travelling or have satisfied a want of nature or have cohabited with a woman and can find no water, then betake yourselves to pure earth, passing with it lightly over your face and your hands. Surely God is All-Relenting, All-Forgiving (4:43).

ALCOHOL AND GAMBLING IS FORBIDDEN

O YOU who have attained to faith! Intoxicants, games of chance, idolatrous sacrifices at altars, and divining arrows are all abominations, the handiwork of Satan. So, turn wholly away from it that you may attain to true success. By intoxicants and games of chance Satan only desires to create enmity and hatred among you, and to turn you away from the remembrance of God and from Prayer. Will you, then, desist (5:90-91)?

OBSERVE PRAYERS AND PAY ZAKAT (CHARITY)

E stablish Prayer from the declining of the sun to the darkness of the night and hold fast to the recitation of the Quran at dawn, for the recitation of the Quran at dawn is witnessed (17:78).

And rise from sleep during the night as well- this is an additional Prayer for you. Possibly your Lord will raise you to an honored position. And pray: "My Lord! Cause me to enter wherever it be, with Truth, and cause me to exit, wherever it be, with Truth, and support me with authority from Yourself (17:79-80)."

Establish Prayer and pay Zakah and obey the Messenger so that mercy may be shown to you. Do not even imagine that those who disbelieve can render God powerless in the land. Their abode is the Fire; what an evil abode (24:56-57)!

(O Prophet), recite the Book that has been revealed to you and establish Prayer. Surely Prayer forbids indecency and evil. And Allah's remembrance is of even greater merit. God knows all that you do (29:45).

IT DOES NOT MATTER WHAT NAME YOU CALL HIM

Say to them (O prophet!): Call upon Him as God or call upon Him as al-Rahman; call Him by whichever name you will, all His names are beautiful. Neither offer your Prayer in too loud a voice, nor in a voice too low; but follow a middle course." And say: "All praise be to God Who has neither taken to Himself a son, nor has He any partner in His kingdom, nor does He need anyone, out of weakness, to protect Him." So, glorify Him in a manner worthy of His glory (17:110-111).

O YOU who have attained to faith! when the call for Prayer is made on Friday, hasten to the remembrance of God and give up all trading. That is better for you, if you only knew. But when the Prayer is ended, disperse in the land and seek Allah's Bounty, and remember God much so that you may prosper (62:9-10).

LIFE OF THIS WORLD IS MADE TO LOOK GOOD

Worldly life has been made attractive to those who have denied the Truth. Such men deride the men of faith, but the pious shall rank higher than them on the Day of Resurrection. As for worldly livelihood, God grants it to whomsoever He wills without measure (2:212).

CHARITY IS MANDATORY

O YOU who have attained to faith! Spend out of what We have provided you before there comes a Day when there will be no buying and selling, nor will friendship and intercession be of any avail. Indeed, those who disbelieve are the wrong-doers (2:254).

O you who have attained to faith! Do not nullify your acts of charity by stressing your benevolence and causing hurt as does he who spends his wealth only to be seen by people and does not believe in God and the Last Day. The example of his spending is that of a rock with a thin coating of earth upon it: when a heavy rain smites it, the earth is washed away, leaving the rock bare; such people derive no gain from their acts of charity. God does not set the deniers of the Truth on the Right Way (2:264).

BE CLEAR IN YOUR HEART ABOUT THE TRUTH

Do not be like those who fell into factions and became opposed to one another after Clear Signs had come to them. A mighty chastisement awaits them on the Day when some faces will turn bright and other faces will turn dark. Those whose faces have turned dark will be told: "Did you fall into unbelief after you had been blessed with belief? Taste, then, chastisement for your unbelief." And those whose faces have turned bright, they will be in the mercy of God, and therein they shall abide (3:105-107).

USURY AND INTEREST ON
LOANS ARE FORBIDDEN

O YOU who have attained to faith! Do not devour interest, doubled and redoubled, and be mindful of God so that you may attain true success. And do not fear the Fire that awaits those who deny the Truth (3:130-131).

GOD ALONE WHO GRANTS LIFE AND DEALS DEATH

O you who have attained to faith! do not be like those who disbelieved and said to their brethren (who met some suffering) in the course of journey or fighting: "Had they remained with us, they would not have died nor been slain." God makes such thoughts the cause of deep regrets in their hearts. For in truth it is God alone who grants life and deals death. God sees all that you do (3:156).

Do to grieve for the deniers of Truth

Let not those who run towards unbelief grieve you; they shall not hurt God in the least. God will not provide for them any share in the Next Life. A mighty chastisement awaits them (3:176).

THERE ARE SIGNS OF HIS MANIFESTATION EVERYWHERE

S urely in the creation of the heavens and the earth, and in the alternation of night and day, there ae Signs for people of understanding - those who remember God while standing, sitting or (reclining) on their backs, and reflect in the creation of the heavens and the earth, (saying): "Our Lord! You have not created this in vain. Glory to You! Save us, then, from the chastisement of the Fire (3:190-191).

PRAYERS

Our Lord! Whomsoever You cause to enter the Fire, him You indeed bring to disgrace, and there will be none to rescue the wrong doers (3:192).

"O our Sustainer! Behold, we heard a voice calling to the faith, saying: "Believe in your Lord"; so we did believe. Our Lord! Forgive us our sins and wipe out our evil deeds and make us die with the truly pious (3:193).

"And, O our Sustainer, grant us that which You have promised us through Your apostles, and disgrace us not on Resurrection Day! Verily, you never fail to fulfil Your promise (3:194)!"

And thus, does their Sustainer answer their prayer: "I shall not lose sight of the labor of any of you who labors [in My way], be it man or woman: each of you is an issue of the other. Hence, as for those who forsake the domain of evil, and are driven from their homelands, and suffer hurt in My cause, and fight [for it], and are slain - I shall most certainly efface their bad deeds, and shall most certainly bring them into gardens through which rivers flow, as a reward from God: for with God is the most beauteous of rewards (3:195)."

Surrender to God

Believers, bow down and prostrate yourselves before your lord and serve your lord and do good that you may prosper. Strive in the cause of God in a manner worthy of that striving. He has chosen you (for his task), and he has not laid upon you any hardship in religion. Keep to the faith of your father Abraham. God named you Muslims earlier and even in this (book), that the messenger may be a witness over you, and that you may be witnesses over all mankind. So, establish prayer, and pay zakah, and hold fast to Allah. He is your protector. What an excellent protector; what an excellent helper (22:77-78)!

Believers! Enter wholly into Islam and do not follow in the footsteps of Satan for he is your open enemy (2:208).

Printed in the United States
By Bookmasters